PASTORAL CARE

OF THE MENTALLY ILL

PASTORAL CARE

OF THE MENTALLY ILL

A Handbook for Pastors

By J. A. Davis

Pastoral Care of the Mentally Ill: A Handbook for Pastors

First published by
Universal Publishers/uPUBLISH.com
USA • 2000

ISBN: 1-58112-715-4

www.upublish.com/books/davisj.htm

This book is dedicated to all of the people from whom I have learned so much whose lives are touched by mental illness.

Acknowledgments

There are many people who deserve thanks in bringing this book to life. I especially want to thank the Rev. Richard A. Crist, psychiatrist Dr. Gregory Teas, and author William Blundell, all of whom read the manuscript and made suggestions relating to their particular fields of expertise. I also want to thank Phebe Swinehart who has read draft after draft and encouraged me to keep working, Cathy Hill, for her support and her sense of humor, and the members of Deeper Walk for their prayer support.

Table of Contents

Preface

Preface

Doris* (not her real name) looked at me with tears in her eyes and pleading in her voice. "Will you please call my pastor and explain to him what bipolar means? He just doesn't get it."

At that moment the first seed was planted that led to this book. After working as a chaplain on hospital psychiatric units for ten years, I have come to realize several things. First, we all know people with psychiatric problems. Secondly, all of us have members of our churches with such problems. And, finally, most pastors have not been trained in working with the mentally ill. Even in the best Clinical Pastoral Education programs, such training is nearly

3

nonexistent.

Let's take a look at a hypothetical 100 families in a hypothetical church. Of these 100 families, it is very likely that there will be at least one person suffering from schizophrenia, one or two suffering from a bipolar (manic-depressive) disorder, ten or so suffering from depression serious enough to warrant medical intervention, perhaps another eight or ten suffering from an addiction or living with someone who does, one or two with eating disorders, and yet another with an obsessive-compulsive problem.

Most of these people at one time or another will be told by someone that they should "talk to their pastor." And that's where this book comes in. What do we tell them? What advice can we give them? How do we keep them safe? And how do we keep from becoming enablers?

Following are some stories–stories of people suffering from mental illness. These cases are composites drawn from the experiences of several people. All of the stories are based in fact and upon experience. It is my hope that through them you will come to see what works–and what doesn't–and what

4

might work and what might not.

Chapter 1

Body Image

Camille was a very pretty girl. At the ripe old age of two, she was featured in an advertisement for a department store chain. More and more jobs were offered and by the time she was thirteen she was an internationally recognized model. Her parents never worried about her extreme thinness. After all, models had to be thin. She was a good student and her tutors kept her up with her classes as she traveled throughout the world.

One day when she was seventeen she came to me and admitted that she had been anorexic and bulimic since she was ten–and addicted to heroin since she was fourteen. She

9

claimed that heroin helped her to control her appetite. However, she was bright enough to know that her addiction and eating disorder would kill her, and she wanted help.

Camille's parents were in denial. Even though she'd been hospitalized briefly for her eating disorder, they didn't really think there was a problem. "It's just because she's so concerned about her career. After all, we all have gone on diets," her mother said. Camille was frightened. Without the support of her parents, she didn't know if she would be able to overcome her problems. She felt very alone. Furthermore, she was ashamed and didn't want anyone to know that anything was wrong; she had an image to maintain. She was the famous Camille–a celebrity in both her school and her church.

Superficially, Ellen seemed an entirely different case. A sophomore in college, she was grossly overweight. One day she called me and asked if we could have lunch. I knew immediately that this wasn't a casual luncheon invitation but an "I've just got to talk to you" lunch. And so, looking at my packed calendar and groaning inwardly, I cheerfully made a date with her for that very day.

As she was eating the last of her double cheeseburger which she was downing with a chocolate shake, she looked at me with the saddest look I've ever seen. Her eyes filled with tears and she blurted out, "Can I tell you something? Something that you can't tell anyone?" I told her that of course she could, and she proceeded to tell me about an uncle who had sexually abused her from age eight to age thirteen. She wailed, "I never want another man anywhere near me. If I stay fat, they'll stay away."

Ellen had every bit as much of an eating disorder as Camille. Camille was obsessed with controlling her figure and her career. Ellen was set on controlling her relationships with men. And they both felt in control as long as they could control how much they ate.

Many people with eating disorders are very controlling people. Often they are compulsively good students and real neatniks. They are obsessive about their eating patterns just as they are obsessive about studying, about getting straight "A's," about being perfect. Often they are trying to please a parent—one that they will probably never please.

11

Sandy was like that. She just wanted her dad to praise her. She got all "A's" and played on the winning varsity volleyball team. When she was elected captain, her dad's comment was, "I would have been disappointed if they hadn't elected you." When she made National Honor Society, her father said, "It's just what we expected of you."

Sandy started exercising. Soon she was exercising eight hours a night–sleeping little, eating less. She got thinner and thinner. She began to find that eating even a little food was making her feel guilty–and that throwing up after she ate eased the guilt. And so a pattern developed; she binged, she purged, she exercised, and she felt in control.

For a while Sandy wore big baggy sweaters that covered up her increasing boniness–but then summer came. When she put on shorts and tee-shirts, it was apparent that she had become shockingly thin. It was then her mother called and invited me to have lunch.

As she picked at her luncheon salad–without dressing– Sandy's pencil thin mom told me of her daughter's behavior. As she sipped her diet drink, she told me that she couldn't imagine why Sandy was so obsessed with what she ate. I suggested that perhaps she was trying to be like Mom, but had gotten a little carried away. It was obviously time for Sandy to have a complete physical examination and probably some long term counseling. I stressed to her mother the seriousness of anorexia, telling her very pointedly that some people actually starve themselves to death.

Eating disorders are especially common among teenage girls and young adult women. However, they are not limited to young people, as witnessed by Sandy's mom. Compulsive eating behavior goes way beyond a teen's desire to be attractive, as we see in Ellen's case. Her obesity, Camille's anorexia and heroin addiction, and Sandy's anorexia and bulimia, are all life-threatening illnesses.

Although most people with eating disorders are women, men are not immune. Bill was an obsessive-compulsive perfectionist. He used to be a really big eater. He was a chubby child who grew into a chubby adult. When he reached 265 pounds, a doctor who was seeing him for the first time told him, "Lose 100 pounds–and I don't care how you do it." Bill was a person who was always anxious to please. He had

13

spent his life trying to please his father without succeeding. He went on a crash diet. He ate nothing but fish and green vegetables and lost a lot of weight. But Bill really missed the large pizzas that he used to eat all by himself. And so one night he ordered one, ate it, got sick–and discovered bingeing and purging. From that point on he threw up every meal he ate.

At that point Bill was also abusing thyroid medication. He was completely obsessed with becoming thin. He eventually lost 135 pounds and looked like someone who had been in a concentration camp. Then he went into heart failure. He was hospitalized in a medical unit for several days and then became irrational and belligerent; he had developed a toxic psychosis from the excessive consumption of thyroid medication. His wife called her pastor to ask what she should do. He volunteered to take her to the hospital so that she could transfer Bill to a locked psychiatric unit in another hospital, as his doctors had recommended. The staff made it clear that she wasn't "committing" him, but Bill became angry, hostile, and threatening. As he begged her to take him home, her pastor gently took her by the arm saying, "It's time to leave," and led her out of the hospital.

People with eating disorders are often easier to spot than those with other mental illnesses because of the physical characteristics manifested by these disorders. Extreme thinness almost to the point of emaciation (when the person does not have some serious medical condition that might lead to this state) or extreme and increasing obesity can be symptoms. However, we must be careful because some people are just thin and wiry, or heavier than most. To assume that all people with these physical characteristics have an eating disorder is as bad as closing our eyes to the disorder.

For example, Sarah, an adult, weighed only seventy-nine pounds. She told me that whenever her family was transferred to a new place, every new doctor she found always assumed that something was wrong with her. Nothing was; she was healthy, ate normally, and was just thin–probably due to genetics. Fred, on the other hand, is quite round. So are his sister, and his cousin, and one of his children. They are all healthy. He explained to me once that diets didn't work for any of them because their metabolisms adjusted so efficiently to having less food. His other sibling and three other children are of what we would call "normal" weight.

15

Pastoral care in the case of folks with eating disorders frequently doesn't take place until the person has reached a crisis point, often hospitalization, as in the case of Camille and Bill. However, it is often a non-family member who will first notice the signs of dysfunction. Family members see other family members every day. It is difficult to notice weight loss or gain from day to day. Pastors may see these same folks weekly or, in some cases, less often. The change will be more noticeable.

If a teen becomes painfully thin and eats only lettuce at the church potluck, it's appropriate to gently ask the parents if their child has been ill–that she looks so thin. They truly might not have noticed; anorexics and bulimics are very clever at hiding their weight loss and their eating habits. The problem is compounded by the hectic pace of modern life; fewer families eat meals together now.

Generally, it is a crisis that brings the patient to you. He or she may ask to meet you for lunch, as Ellen did, or perhaps a parent, spouse or sibling will seek your counsel. When you learn of the problem, it is extremely important that you make clear that this is a life-threatening illness and that a doctor should be seen immediately.

Clinical Considerations

Though men can suffer eating disorders, they are much more common in women than in men. Many girls develop them during early adolescence when they are trying to learn who they are. However, eating disorders have been diagnosed in younger children and in older adults. Some of the psychological issues that influence the development of eating disorders include low self-esteem, control issues, having unrealistically high expectations, a desire to please or to get attention, or, in the case of obesity, sexual abuse of some sort. Often eating disorders are accompanied by depression, substance abuse, or severe anxiety.

Anorexia and bulimia can lead to heart problems, erosion of tooth enamel, cessation of menstruation, dehydration, anemia, osteoporosis, and other serious conditions. Extreme obesity may strain the heart, elevate blood pressure, limit mobility, and trigger back and joint pain. None of these conditions is to be taken lightly. They are not just eating patterns, but rather an obsession with food. Again, any of these disorders can be

17

life threatening and even fatal. Anorexia alone has a fifteen percent early death rate.

It is never easy to tell a friend or a parishioner that he or she needs help. However, most of us are not trained to deal with problems of this magnitude, and gently asking if the person has thought about entering into therapy, stressing the benefits of a therapeutic relationship in whatever the case may be, is something that family members or others close to the person may simply not have the nerve to do. And so, because people are told to talk to their clergyperson, it is up to you to not only pray with and for them, but to refer them to the professional help they need.

When someone is hospitalized for one of these disorders, what this person needs is not advice. He is getting that from his doctors and therapists. What he needs to experience in your visit is God's unconditional love. We are not called to diagnose, or to tell people how to get well. We are there to remind them that they are important parts of the body of Christ, to love them, and to listen to them and hear what they are—and what they are not—saying.

Many people with eating disorders will be hospitalized. I would not recommend visiting at mealtimes, because those times are a great source of stress and embarrassment. The meals of patients being treated for eating disorders are closely monitored and recorded. It is also not a good idea to visit right after meals, because for those who are bulimic, that, too, is a time of great stress because they are not permitted to be out of sight of hospital staff. They are used to throwing up their food and do not feel in control when someone else is watching them. At other times your visit may be welcomed. Even then, however, they often do not want others in the church to know anything about their illness. They may be embarrassed because in their attempt to control, they have lost control. Or they may ask you to talk with their family members and explain what they are going through. Each case is as individual as the person involved.

The important thing is that the person be visited, and that pastoral support be offered. The illness need not be discussed unless the patient brings it up. Perhaps the best approach is to assure the person that she is missed and to talk about what is going on in the body of Christ in her absence. In addition, you might want to offer prayers for strength and healing.

19

Chapter 2

Highs and Lows

I first met Susan the second day I worked at the hospital.
One of the nurses had suggested that I go in and talk with
her. I knocked on her door. She mumbled, "Yeah. What?" I
went in and introduced myself, telling her that Jane had
suggested that she might like to talk to me. Acting her
toughest, she said, "Fine. Okay. But don't give me any of the
God stuff." And that's where we started.

Susan was an attractive, if somewhat overweight, young
woman of nineteen. She had gang signs tattooed on her
hands, nine earrings in each ear, and angry red cuts on her
arms and legs. We talked a little about mundane things–the

temperature on the locked unit, hospital food, and how much she was sleeping. I didn't bring up "the God stuff."

After a while, Susan must have decided that I was okay because I wasn't preaching at her. She got friendlier and started to tell me a little about herself. An alcoholic and cocaine addict, she was a member of a street gang. Bipolar (manic depressive), Susan was psychotic and hearing voices. She lacked self esteem and had a tragic family history; her mother had died after a long illness when Susan was in high school and she had been physically and sexually abused by a family member. She had a baby when she was fifteen.

During the ensuing days of her hospital stay, she told me more. She had made a number of serious suicide attempts. The voices she heard told her that she was useless, no good to anyone. They told her over and over that the best thing she could do was to kill herself. To try to stop the pain of her illness and to stop the voices, she cut her arms and legs with knives or razor blades and burned her abdomen with cigarettes. She said that the physical pain stopped the mental anguish, if only for a while.

When Susan was eight, she had been hit by a motorcycle and her legs were seriously injured. She was in casts for months and her oldest brother began torturing her and sexually abusing her. This went on for years, because, true to the pattern of sexual abusers, he threatened her life if she told anyone.

In high school, while trying to deal with her mother's cancer, which preoccupied the whole family, she found another family in a street gang. She even thought the gang could protect her from her brother. The gang affiliation quickly led to involvement in drugs and sexual acting out. One of these sexual encounters led to the baby born when Susan was just fifteen. It was given up for adoption.

Susan was not a child of poverty. In fact, she was from a wealthy, upper-middle class family and lived in a "classy" suburb of a big city. The family regularly attended church services and gave generously of their time and money to the church. But Susan got lost in the shuffle. She was the youngest child of nine and, as she was the only one left at home when her mother's cancer spread, she was the one who tended her. Her father was in such denial of the mother's

25

condition that he essentially did nothing for her, and all the responsibility fell on Susan. Her siblings were older and starting their own families, "too busy" to help. And so Susan, who once was a straight "A" student, cut classes, ran with the gang instead, got arrested from time to time, started drinking and doing drugs, and grieved for her mother's deteriorating health.

Who knows what pastoral intervention might have done? But it didn't happen. After her mother died, Susan stopped going to church. Grief support was focused on her father, leaving Susan to try to sort things out on her own. She couldn't understand why her mother had died in the prime of life. It was all so painful that she began to drink and use cocaine regularly to dull the pain. But the pain wouldn't go away. It was then she began injuring herself. The suicide attempts followed; on one occasion she overdosed with her brother's medication and almost died. She was in a coma for several days. Finally, she got psychiatric help.

Susan had been a "mistake" baby—one that came ten years after her youngest sibling. She was alternately a pest or a plaything to her brothers and sisters. Her parents were tired from raising eight other children. They foisted her off on her older siblings who, of course, resented both the attention she got and the work for them that she represented. Once she was hit by the motorcycle, she was even more of a problem to them. And, as children will do, they made no secret of their feelings. So the self-image she grew up with was, "I'm a mistake, I'm a problem, I'm a nuisance, everyone would be happier if I hadn't been born." Add this to her bipolar illness and her mother's death and it's no wonder she joined a gang and got into trouble.

Part of the manifestation of bipolar illness includes reckless spending. One day, with a credit card in hand, Susan bought eleven portable AM-FM stereos and gave them away in the parking lot of a mall. She thought if she gave people things then maybe they would like her and she'd be worth something in their eyes. She didn't know that she was a beloved child of God and that God's love was unconditional. She was too focused on trying to earn love from somewhere else. "But this didn't work," she told me tearfully. "People just thought I was crazy. So I started looking for love in sex. That didn't work either. They just used me." Her eyes welled up with tears. "You're a pastor. I'm a horrible person. Why do you

27

even bother talking to me?" I was tempted to jump right in with stories of God's unconditional love, to say that Susan was one of God's children and that Jesus commanded us to love one another. But she had made the rules at the beginning: none of that God stuff. Now that she was opening up, I didn't want to lose her, so I just smiled and said, "Because I care about you." Meanwhile, I was praying that God's love would shine through me and that eventually she'd put two and two together.

I did not judge. I did not show shock at her sometimes raw language. I just listened. And I really did care. I saw a spark behind the toughness. I saw potential. But most of all, I saw one of God's children.

Susan was in and out of the hospital eight times that year. Usually she was admitted in serious condition, hallucinating, hearing voices, and often once again having tried to kill herself. I spent a lot of time talking with her, encouraging her, and believing in her worth as a human being.

Susan's family rarely visited. A friend or two might, but not often. She felt lonely and abandoned. The people who knew her best and cared most about her were those of us who worked in the hospital. Even though her family was still active and involved in their church, no one from the church visited her–a situation all too familiar in psychiatric hospitals. Either the patient is ashamed of being there and tells no one–often the case because of the stigma of mental illness in our society–or people are afraid to visit because they don't know what to expect. Or, in many cases, the pastor makes an attempt to visit and is told that the patient is unavailable because of scheduled activities. Sometimes attempts at pastoral visits are not encouraged because involvement in religion is thought of as part of the problem and clergy are thought by staff to be meddling. Whatever the case, the patient is isolated from the very support he or she needs.

Through therapy, Susan eventually stopped drinking and doing drugs. When she finally stayed out of the hospital for a time and became somewhat stable on a large number of medications, she decided one Sunday to come to the church where I was on staff. Perhaps she wanted me to see her outside of the hospital setting. Perhaps she came because she was curious. Perhaps she came because God nudged her and something deep within her responded. Whatever it was that

29

brought her there got her there more than once.

Our congregation had been educated about mental illness. In the days when patients would stay in the hospital for two or three weeks, members of the adult Sunday school wrote notes of encouragement to them. They knew only their first names and that they were patients in a mental health unit. They wrote to them and they prayed for them. I took the letters to the patients when I went to do services on Sunday afternoons. It was a powerful experience for both writer and recipient. Therefore, when Susan came to church, had the congregation known of her illness, it would not have made any difference.

Susan and I continued to talk, and one day I suggested to her that she take some classes at the local community college. She protested that no one would like her, that no one would even talk to her, and that she couldn't afford it anyway. I suggested that she apply for financial aid. I also told her that she was a very likeable person and that I knew she wouldn't have any problems.

A few months later she called me and asked if I would help

her fill out the financial aid paperwork. I was delighted and made an appointment to meet with her the next day. We got the paperwork done and sent in and, lo and behold, she got the aid she needed–tuition and books! However, because her family was unwilling to offer any help at all, she had no appropriate clothes to wear. And so the church provided gift certificates for clothes through the generosity of several people who provide ongoing anonymous funds for just such things.

She got involved in school, studied hard, took her medications regularly, got straight A's, and was only hospitalized three times during her two-year program. She graduated with honors and got a job in the field she had studied.

I'd love to say that she lived happily ever after, but that's not the nature of bipolar illness. At some point the job became very stressful, her family became very demanding, she stopped taking her medication, and once again was hearing voices telling her to kill herself. She came to see me and talked and talked about having no reason to live. By this time in our relationship, we had talked about the "God stuff" and she knew that I prayed for her every day. I told her that she was one of God's children and that she was loved, but that didn't seem to be enough. I'd run out of things to say. And then God gave me a wonderful gift–the gift of tears. As I sat there with tears running down my face, she said "If you care that much about what happens to me, then I guess I should go to the hospital." And we called her doctor and I drove her to the hospital.

Susan will never have a life free of mental illness. Often people with bipolar disorder (and other chemical imbalances) stop taking their medications because they don't like the side effects or because of the almost prohibitive cost of many of the medications. The result of getting off of medication is hopefully hospitalization and not suicide.

Susan is older now and has found several reasons to live. First of all, she *knows* that God loves her. Her needs have been provided for when logic said otherwise. People she doesn't know have helped her. Prayers have been answered in dramatic ways from finding her an apartment to finding her a job.

Her relationships with her family are still rocky, but she doesn't let it bother her. She accepts family members as they are, loves them, and doesn't let them get to her. She knows now what she needs to do to take care of herself, and she does it because she has finally learned to love herself.

Susan is working part-time and living in subsidized housing. She will probably never be able to work full time or to fully support herself. Social Security disability payments help her live as a reasonably independent, productive member of society. She meets with a therapist weekly and her psychiatrist monthly. Her medication must be monitored to make sure that her doses don't become toxic. But she has taken responsibility for her life and God is a big part of that life. She knows from whence her help comes.

Clinical Considerations and Pastoral Concerns

Bipolar disorder usually shows up in adolescence or early adulthood. There is no cure for this disease. It will continue throughout the patient's life. There are, however, effective treatments available for bipolar disorder. This disorder tends to run in families. The disorder is characterized by periods of mania and periods of depression. In a manic state the patient may be energetic, not sleep, spend wildly and irresponsibly, be restless, talk rapidly, abuse drugs, and act out sexually. The manic state causes the patient to feel euphoric and to deny that anything is wrong, or to feel paranoid and angry.

I worked with someone suffering from a bipolar disorder and never knew it until stresses in her life caused her to have problems. Her mother was dying and she broke up with her long-term boyfriend. She began having a difficult time at work and so consulted with her psychiatrist who adjusted her medication. As chaplain, I met with her and talked about her losses and offered the sort of care I would offer any other person going through such traumatic times. It is important not to blame situational depression on the illness.

In a depressive state the patient may feel hopeless, helpless, and worthless. He or she may lose interest in doing anything –even getting out of bed or eating. Concentration may be difficult and there may be changes in sleep patterns, often involving excessive sleeping. The person may gain or lose weight. Thoughts of death and suicide are common, as are actual attempts at suicide.

34

Bipolar patients can be very perceptive and often very paranoid. If a clergy person is just "going through the motions" and doesn't really care, the person will pick up on that very quickly. Working with people like Susan takes a great deal of patience. When bipolar people are in a depressive state, they have a very hard time believing that anyone could possibly care about them. They must be convinced. Furthermore, bipolar illness is not a short term problem that will go away. Although current medications go a long way in controlling symptoms, they do not *cure* the illness. Loss, extreme stress, physical health issues, and financial problems may well trigger a setback.

Often people with bipolar disorder do not realize that they need help. When they do approach us for help, they should be encouraged to see a mental health professional and, in some cases, must be taken for treatment for their own protection.

Chapter 3

Really Down

Glenn approached me one day on the way out of church. "Do you have some time this week that you could come over to our house and talk to Claudia and me? We're worried about Amy." From the look on his face, I decided that something serious was going on and that "some time this week" had better be soon. I told them that I could see them the next evening.

When I got to their home, they skipped the usual pleasantries and got right to the point. "Amy has been cutting herself. She does it where no one can see it–on her breasts and on her stomach. We just don't understand. What have we done

39

wrong? WHY is she doing this?" Their words came tumbling out and their anguish was evident.

These people were solid church members. Their daughter Amy and their son David had been raised in the church and were active in Sunday School and in the high school youth group. They were good kids who had gotten through high school with no more than the usual problems and were now both in college.

Amy was a musician. She had played violin since fourth grade and was hoping to be a professional musician when she graduated. She was very talented–perhaps not exceptional, but certainly very good. She did have a fallback plan; she had a minor in library science, but her first love was her music.

And speaking of love, she had a boyfriend. They had gone together for three years. He was about to graduate and she had one more year to go, so they were facing a major separation. This put stress on their relationship; Amy had broken up with him twice. Yet each time she did, she felt guilty and lonely and wished that she hadn't severed the relationship.

40

Glenn and Claudia told me all of this and they asked what they should do. They were worried about Amy cutting herself–they simply didn't understand how anyone could do that–but they were also worried about the fact that the "spark" had gone out of her. She seemed to be just existing rather than living.

Amy was obviously depressed. I explained that clinical depression isn't a character flaw but rather a chemical imbalance in the brain, an imbalance treatable with medication. I suggested that therapy might also be indicated to help Amy deal with the many stresses in her life at the time.

Within a week Glenn and Claudia had taken Amy for an evaluation at a nearby hospital with a well-respected psychiatric unit. She was admitted to a four-week outpatient day program where she would get group and individual therapy, and was also put on an antidepressant drug by the psychiatrist.

Amy felt better after the month in the program. Her parents were convinced that she was no longer hurting herself and

41

noticed that she had a renewed interest in life. But, a month before she graduated, a stressful time for anyone, Amy began another downward spiral. She had been trying without success to find a job as a violinist and was getting so discouraged and distraught that her parents once again feared for her safely. Once again they called me and asked me what they should do. I asked if they thought that she was in danger. They weren't sure. I said that if they were concerned about her safety that they should take her to the emergency room at the hospital. Patients who are suicidal will not be turned away. They didn't think she was suicidal, so I suggested that the psychiatrist be contacted immediately for a possible adjustment in medication.

Ultimately the medication was upped, Amy got better, she graduated, and she got a position as a librarian. She is staying in touch with her music by playing in a volunteer community symphony–for now.

The pastoral issues in the case are several. First, the parents were in need of comfort, information, support, and prayer. They put Amy on the prayer chain list, but Amy didn't want anyone to know what was wrong with her. As is so often true, the stigma of mental illness was an issue. Amy didn't want anyone to know that she had been in the hospital outpatient program or that she was seeing a psychiatrist.

Pastoral support of Amy was more difficult. I saw her in the outpatient setting and assured her of confidentiality. I also offered her my listening ear if she ever needed it. When she had her setback before graduation, I gave her reassuring hugs after church services, but never mentioned her illness to her. Because of her desire that no one know, any mention of the situation would have to come from her. It never did.

Glenn and Claudia still talk with me from time to time. I'm the person with whom they can share their fears safely and in confidentiality. And because of my job at the hospital, they see me as their local mental health information source.

Amy's battle is probably not over. But as long as she learns to recognize the signs of the onset of a depressive period, she should be able to live a good life--even though she may need to be on medication the rest of her life.

Various life situations may contribute to the onset of clinical depression. Marie's husband of seventeen years left her. She hadn't seen the break coming and was overwhelmed with the responsibilities of raising two teenage boys, keeping the house running, and staying financially stable. Marie attended church almost daily and each day I saw her changing. First her choice of clothing went from stylish to dark, mismatched sweats. Then she stopped wearing any makeup–not even lipstick. After that she stopped fixing her hair which hung stringily onto her shoulders.

Trying to open the lines of communication, I frequently asked Marie how she was getting along but she would only smile and say, "Well, just fine." But each time she answered her voice became flatter and flatter. Finally one morning there was a message on the answering machine. "This is Marie. Can we talk?" The dead tone in her voice was even more evident on the machine than it had been in person. I called her right back and made an appointment with her for that afternoon.

Marie came into my office looking like she had just gotten out of bed. Her clothes and her hair were disheveled. She sat down and blurted out, "I don't know how I can go on." Then, shoulders shaking, she sobbed and sobbed. When she was cried out and began to talk it was evident that she was seriously depressed over the departure of her husband. I suggested that she might want to talk with a psychologist. I also explained that there is depression that is physical rather than situational.

People who are depressed, whether they are suffering from a bipolar disorder or clinical depression, don't want or need to be told to snap out of it any more than diabetics need to be told to snap out of it. I cringe when I hear people say such things as "What do you have to be depressed about? You have a beautiful home, great kids, a wonderful spouse, and lots of money. What could you *possibly* be depressed about?" Comments such as these come from ignorance, not educated concern. They are harmful because they minimize what is a very real illness. They are as insensitive as saying to a cancer patient "Why are you worried about a little lump? We all have some lumps and bumps."

I told Marie I cared about her but that I didn't feel qualified to deal with the deep issues she was facing. I assured her of my support, telling her I would pray for and with her and be available to her. I made certain that she knew that she could continue to call on me. Then I gave her the names of three psychologists that I respected and who I knew would guide her to a psychiatrist should medication be called for.

Marie was so despondent that she was willing to try anything. She made the appointment, started in therapy with an appropriate professional, got on antidepressant medication, and slowly began to recover. It was a joy to watch her progress, to finally hear a lilt in her voice, and to see her once again taking care of her appearance. I urged her, after a while, to join a small study group at the church, knowing that she needed to reestablish relationships with other adults.

Many years have passed since Marie called my answering machine. She is still a regular church attender, is active in many small groups, both women's groups and mixed groups. She has gone back to school and started a whole new career. Her teenage boys turned out well–with, I might add, good professional counseling to help them deal with their father's abandonment of the family–and are both happily married with several children each. Marie enjoys her career and loves being a grandmother. Occasionally something triggers a return of Marie's depression. She now knows the symptoms and promptly contacts her doctor who prescribes antidepressants for a relatively short period of time. And so she carries on with her life in a generally joyful and upbeat manner.

Marie's faith has always been an important component of her recovery, and her psychologist had to be someone who was understanding of the importance of God in her life. In referring patients, it is important to have some knowledge of where the psychologist stands in the matters of faith. I was told about one psychologist who thought that God was a crutch, all men should have mistresses, and all women should take lovers. The patient seeing that person quickly changed to another counselor with values she could share. It is important to assure people seeking help that if they don't feel after a few sessions that the professional they chose is the right one for them, that they change. A good match is very important.

Clinical and Pastoral Considerations

Depression is probably the most prevalent mental illness, striking one in ten people at some time in their lives. Women are more prone to depression than men, but men are far from immune; according to the National Alliance for the Mentally

47

Ill, one in fifteen men will suffer from major depression at some time in their lives. For women the numbers are one in five. This is a serious as well as widespread illness, but it is a generally a treatable illness, as we can see in the cases of Amy and Marie.

We need to remember that there is a difference between the disorder of major depression and the normal "down times" most people have. It is normal to be sad when someone dies, when one loses a job, when the lack of money becomes a major issue. This depression is a human emotion. The disorder of major depression is a biological disease that, in most cases, is treatable with medication.

The symptoms of depression include hopelessness, sadness that won't go away, emptiness, changes in sleep patterns, difficulty in concentrating, weight loss or gain, lack of interest in doing anything and diminished enjoyment in anything that is attempted. A trip to the grocery store can be overwhelming because of the decisions that must be made. Many depressed people have very low self esteem. They feel they aren't worth much and this prevents them from sticking up for themselves. They're convinced that nothing will ever get better, so they see no reason to try. Often they feel trapped.

Adolescents and children, not just adults, also become depressed. Adolescents may deal with their depression by drinking or taking drugs, by running away, or by attempting suicide. Children act out, are moody, and often can't control their tempers. About three percent of children under thirteen, and thirteen percent of teenagers, suffer from depression, according to the National Mental Health Association.

The classic symptoms of depression in children and teenagers include sleep and appetite problems, concentration difficulties leading to poor school performance, sudden changes of habits, unreasonable fears, and thoughts of death. If a child or teen appears to be unusually sad most of the time and over an extended period, it is very possible that he or she is suffering from major depression.

Parents see their children every day and often don't notice a gradual slide into depression. They tend to think that the child is just being "difficult" or going through a stage. If you have serious concerns about a young person, it could be helpful, and even lifesaving, to approach the parents with those concerns. Use nonthreatening statements such as "I've noticed that Sam doesn't seem to participate in the Sunday School activities and is having a hard time staying focused. Is anything going on there that we can help with or that we should know?" It is not up to you to diagnose, but only to be supportive and alert to what is going on.

Depression is not a respecter of age. The elderly are frequent victims of depression. Elmer, 73, had fallen and seriously injured his back. Gradually he got better, but he was in constant pain. One day, deciding that he was a burden to his wife, he jumped out of a third story window. He didn't die; instead he further injured himself and ended up in a wheelchair.

When I met Elmer, he was so depressed that he could barely talk. He didn't want to live. He had been a printer in his working life so one day I started talking with him about computers and all the fun one can have on them with fonts and layout options. He told me he was too old to learn, that he was finished, and that he just wanted to die. He had been a faithful member of his church all his life, but he felt so guilty about the suicide attempt that he was embarrassed to even talk with his pastor. Elmer was given various oral medications, but nothing seemed to do much good. He still wanted to die. Meanwhile, he was receiving physical therapy for his back, but he wasn't making a lot of progress because he refused to do the exercises.

Finally his psychiatrist recommended electroconvulsive therapy. Elmer reluctantly agreed, secretly hoping that it would kill him. It didn't; he got better. He decided to work on his physical therapy. His desire to die went away. And when I last saw him, the day he was being discharged from the hospital, he was planning to go back to work part-time and to learn all about computer graphics. He had a whole new lease on life. As an added bonus, his back pain had nearly gone away.

Too often people think that depression is a natural part of aging. It isn't. Many people in their 90's and beyond are living active, fun-filled lives. Edith is ninety-five, healthy, bright, active in the church, loves to travel and go out to eat, delights in her grandchildren and great-grandchildren, and is an avid fan of her college football team. She enjoys shopping, gardening, reading, boating, and getting together with friends.

She serves on the governing board of the church and participates in the annual women's retreat as well as a book group and a dinner group. Edith has had the normal losses that someone her age might expect to have. Her husband of sixty-seven years died when they both were ninety and the loss was difficult. But her attitude was, "I can sit around and mourn or I can get on with my life. I think he'd rather that I got on with my life." The next year she and her daughter traveled to London and Paris and two years later they took a trip to Italy. Edith is *not* depressed. She enjoys each and every day.

Grieving statistics show about eighty percent of those still grieving at one year after a serious loss will not be recovered one or two years later. This is not normal grief. A referral to a grief counselor or psychiatrist would be helpful and appropriate. Edith grieved normally and her quality of life has not been diminished.

There are many older people who are bright, alert, and healthy–and there are those who suffer from depression, just like their younger friends. Their depression is usually treatable with medication–Elmer was an extreme example–

but sometimes they don't receive the medication that they need because family members assume they are depressed simply because they are old. Once again, intervention might be in order. "Elmer seems really depressed and withdrawn. Have you mentioned this to his doctor?" This may be all his family needs to become aware of the situation.

We are often among those best able to help because people generally will at least listen to what we say. So, be direct with your parishioners when you suspect a problem with depression, whether the person is five or ninety-five. Help is available. No one need suffer from this debilitating disorder.

Chapter 4

Hearing Voices

Mildred's voice was stressed–in fact I could barely hear her. "He tried to kill me–my son tried to kill me." She was calling from the hospital. Her twenty-three year old schizophrenic son thought that she was an alien spy and tried to choke her. What precipitated this attack? She asked him if he had taken his medication.

Tom's problems had begun when he was nineteen. He was away at college and ended up in the hospital. Tom was an honor student–salutatorian of his high school class. He had gone away to a prestigious university and it was there that he had his first psychotic break. He started hearing voices and thought people were talking about him and plotting against him. To try to stop the voices, he would drive all night with his stereo blasting–but the voices got louder and louder. He finally was hospitalized when he refused to get dressed for days and accused his roommate of being a foreign spy.

Tom came home from college and was hospitalized for several months. He was placed on a variety of medications which made the voices less frequent and less loud, but he hated the side effects. They made him tired, like a zombie, he said. Some made his face and neck stiff, but he took them for a while. He stayed home with Mildred and worked part time moving boxes in a warehouse.

One day Tom left work without explanation. He was found 160 miles from home, disoriented, out of gasoline, and out of money. Mildred called her good friend from church who drove her to where Tom was stranded so that she could drive his car back.

Tom continued to live at home, working from time to time, until the night he attacked his mother. At one point during the attack, when he had her pinned to the ground, a flicker of recognition passed through his head and he said "You're hurt. We'd better call someone." She escaped from his grasp and called 911.

When the police came, they arrested Tom and took Mildred to the hospital. Tom subsequently spent a year and a half in the state mental hospital. When Mildred was released from the hospital, she had a security system installed in her home and an order of protection issued so her son couldn't come to her house.

When Tom was released from the state hospital, he began living in a group home monitored by the county. They made sure that he took his medications, giving them by injection. (One of the main problems in treating schizophrenia is the tendency of patients to stop taking their medications. They presume that because they are feeling better, they don't need to continue any longer.)

Tom has been back in various hospitals a number of times. At one point his voices were telling him that he needed to touch people. Obviously this kind of behavior doesn't work well in society. When I visited him in the hospital, he suddenly stood up, let out a guttural moan, and came toward me. I was visiting with him in the day room with other patients and staff members present, so his actions were interrupted by staff members. Remember that psychiatric patients can be very unpredictable and that it is a good idea, when visiting in the hospital, to tell a staff member where you are.

Another time Tom was working in a sheltered workshop. He was convinced that the sounds coming out of the intercom were messages from secret agents of the government who were telling him that other workers were dangerous spies. The voices that severe schizophrenics hear are very real to them and can cause them to do harm to themselves or others. They need to be monitored on medication. Also, pastoral care professionals should be aware that the patient who is docile and friendly one minute may turn on them–or on anyone–the next.

The pastoral issues here are primarily ones of support and understanding. Mildred was visited in the hospital and offers were made to visit Tom, but he didn't want his pastor to see him in "that place." When Tom had a Sunday pass, Mildred, accompanied by a friend, brought him to church. The task

60

facing the pastor in such a situation is to be friendly and welcoming to this person, who now may barely resemble the carefree young man who grew up in the church.

Clinical Considerations

Schizophrenia usually strikes young adults between the ages of seventeen and twenty-five. It is a biochemical disorder of the brain and is not caused by how the person was raised or by any other environmental factor; drug abuse or alcohol abuse does not cause schizophrenia. It is a *disease,* every bit as much as cancer or heart disease. There is no known preventive and no known cure. However, today's medications can often control the symptoms so that the patient can live an almost normal life.

About a third of schizophrenic patients who are diagnosed and hospitalized will recover completely and another third will be significantly improved, needing only occasional hospitalization. The other third will not respond to current therapies and will remain quite ill. Tom falls somewhere between the last two categories. He will always have to live in a group home, but he is able to work in a sheltered workshop much of the time.

Most schizophrenics do best living away from home in an atmosphere of calm and quiet. Though they like to be around people from time to time, large groups are difficult for them. Strong emotion can be overwhelming to them, and humor is beyond many who are suffering from schizophrenia.

Schizophrenic delusions can cause violence. Delusions are untrue ideas that the patient believes are true. Patients having paranoid delusions believe that they are being watched or followed or persecuted, and may attack someone in what they perceive as self-defense. Others believe that they are powerful political or religious figures. One in my hospital wore a white robe, had long hair and a beard, and was convinced that he was Jesus. Most untreated schizophrenics have hallucinations—usually auditory but sometimes visual, or a combination of the two. They may think that their body parts have lives of their own. Logical thinking is beyond them.

Changes in emotional response may signal the onset of schizophrenia. The person may develop unreasonable fears or inappropriate responses to emotions; he or she may seem to be "slowed down" and withdrawn and may be suspected of abusing drugs. Withdrawal is common because outside stimuli become too much for schizophrenics to handle.

Pastoral Concerns

Schizophrenia is a tragic disease with effects on the entire family. To watch a formerly bright and articulate young person turn into a withdrawn, paranoid young adult is heartbreaking for parents and siblings. Often a patient who is quite ill, such as Tom, will need a lifetime of custodial care. Pastoral support of both family and patient are extremely important. The patient should be treated as we would treat anyone–with the love of Christ. Family members will need to feel included and loved, not blamed. Congregations should be educated about mental illness so that they understand the causes of schizophrenia and no longer have an unreasoning fear of those suffering from it. Families should be guided to organizations such as the National Alliance for the Mentally Ill, which has local chapters in many places. They offer information and support for people trying to deal with the mental illness of a family member.

Chapter 5

General Conclusions

We've met some people who have some very real problems.
These problems, however, do not keep them from loving
God, from seeking companionship with others who love God.
They sing in our choirs, they serve on our committees, they
worship with us most every Sunday. Some are married.
Some are single. Some have families. Most have jobs. All are
God's children. All have mental illnesses.

There is so much misunderstanding and stigma connected
with mental illness that people suffering from one of these
diseases need to know that they are loved and supported by
their church community. Congregations need to be educated

about mental illness and learn that mentally ill parishioners are every bit as much in need of loving care as are those suffering from other physical diseases. They need to be included. People must learn not to fear them. Often they have gotten their information from stereotypical representations in movies or on television. People must understand that they probably know and work with those who are mentally ill and don't even know it.

Telling a parishioner that he or she might benefit from a visit to a therapist or psychiatrist is not an easy thing to do. Often people seek guidance from pastors, pastoral counselors, and chaplains when they are troubled. It is important to know when we are in over our heads and when the person might be a danger to himself or others. One tactful way to approach this matter of referral is to say something like this: "You know, I think I'm in a little over my head here. It might be really helpful for you to talk to someone else. A couple of people I know of that are really good are (then make referrals —with phone numbers.)" And then follow up. See if the person has followed through. Continue to show loving concern, but don't be moved into the role of therapist if you're not trained for it. We all can be compassionate friends and listeners, but mentally ill people need the expertise of mental health professionals. In order to have a good list of referrals, check with chaplains of mental health facilities or psychiatric nurses. These professionals know which doctors and therapists are sympathetic to the spirituality of patients

It is very important not to get drawn into a patient's illness in an unhealthy way. We can be loving and caring and know when to say, "I think you need to check in with your doctor" or "I think this is a matter for your therapist." I have heard patients call their pastors from the hospital eight or ten times a day. This is not healthy for either pastor or patient. When people are becoming clingingly dependent, we must be wise and discerning. There is a fine line between being firm and being rejecting. Again, I must stress, *refer.* That is the kindest, most loving thing we can do for a person with mental illness.

We must realize sometimes God's children get sick. Diabetics have times of unstable blood sugar and may take insulin daily; people with high blood pressure may have to take daily medications. Those suffering from mental illnesses are no different. They may have flare-ups and require hospitalization–just as diabetics or people with heart conditions or stomach problems may require hospitalization from time to time. When a mentally ill person is having an especially hard time, it is good to ask if any help is needed. Often it is close friends who note the first symptoms of a decline. However, it is not a kindness to ask people if they are taking their medication when they seem to be experiencing problems. This could make them feel like we view them as abnormal. The mentally ill should be allowed to have normal, human emotions without others immediately assuming that they are having a relapse. None of these people are ill because they are bad people. They are ill because they are sick. Our treatment of them all comes back to loving one another, to treating one another in the way we would like to be treated. We have in Jesus Christ as example of how to treat the sick among us–with compassion and love and prayer. In James 5:14-15 we read "Are any among you sick? They should call for the elders of the church and have them pray over them, anointing them with oil in the name of the Lord. The prayer of faith will save the sick, and the Lord will raise them up." The sick need the prayers of the church. Our Lord didn't shun those who were possessed by demons or who had fevers or leprosy. He didn't shun anyone. Yet ignorance and misunderstanding often make people shun those who are mentally ill.

Not only must we, as the body of Christ, reach out to these children of God, but we must do all in our power to educate our congregations so that they will do the same. This does not at all mean violating the confidence of our brothers and sisters afflicted with mental illness but rather educating our people to love and accept all sorts and conditions of humankind.

Many churches have substance abuse groups that meet in their buildings. There are also a large number of groups that deal with mental illness–both support groups for the mentally ill and support groups for their families. Perhaps hosting one of these groups would be a starting place for educating your congregation and helping to remove the stigma that mentally ill people live with every day of their lives.

In the meantime, we, as leaders of the church, can treat every mentally ill person with the same love, concern, and respect with which we treat every other person we encounter. We must not be afraid of them. We must avoid labels and ill-chosen expressions. Often an innocent remark such as "I was really feeling schizophrenic" (meaning double minded) or talking about "a real nut case" or someone being "looney" can have devastating effects on someone who is mentally ill. They will turn you off and not hear anything else you say. These expressions should be considered as inappropriate as racial slurs and sexist remarks. They only hurt people.

We should be as comfortable talking with people about their depression as we are talking with them about their broken leg. If Joe is having a particularly difficult time and is in a deep depression we should be as willing to talk about it with him as we are to talk to Mary about how cumbersome her leg cast is. If Fred has pneumonia and Sally has had a psychotic break, we must minister to them with equal confidence, love, and concern.

It is important to remember that most mentally ill persons lead normal lives. They have families, jobs, and, incidentally, must take medication every day–just like millions of other people. Let us not contribute to the problem by being judgmental or afraid.

The National Alliance for the Mentally Ill (NAMI) has a help line available for patients, families, and all others seeking information or help. That number is 1-800-950-NAMI (1-800-950-6264.) With 1200 state and local affiliates, they stand ready to help and to educate. Their address is NAMI, Colonial Place Three, 2107 Wilson Blvd. 3rd Floor, Arlington, VA 22201. I encourage you to contact them if you seek further information.

May God bless you as you seek to offer compassionate care to those suffering from mental illness and to educate your flock to do the same.

Notes

Printed in the United States
129686LV00001B/182/A